Burgundy & Alsace Travel Guide

Attractions, Eating, Drinking, Shopping & Places To Stay

Brandon Kavanagh

Table of Contents

Welcome to Burgundy

Burgundy is a hilly area of eastern France that is known for its diverse selection of wines. The region starts just south of Dijon with the Côte d'Or, which in itself is divided into two separate areas; Côte de Nuits to the north and Côte de Beaune to the South. The northern part is named after the town of Nuits-St-Georges and is renowned for its red wines. Joined to the Côte d'Or is Côte Chalonnaise, Mâconnais and Beaujolais. The area of Chablis sits on its own to the west.

60,000 acres of land are in use for wine production from which comes some 200 million bottles of wine. This is split into one-third red wine and two-thirds white wine. I am sure most of us are familiar with bottles of Beaune (medium-body red wine) and Chablis (dry white wine) but you should also try the Corton and Pommard (full-bodied reds). Two grapes are primarily used for wine production in Burgundy; Chardonnay (white) and Pinot Noir (red). Other grapes in use are: Gamay (Beaujolais), St-Bris (Sauvignon Blanc) and Bouzeron (Aligoté).

Wines are classified into the appellation system which includes the Grand Cru and the Premier Cru along with village wines and sub-village wines. There are approximately 40 Grand Cru vineyards in Chablis and the Côte d'Or. While the sub-village appellations are at the bottom of the list with careful selection it is possible to find some decent wines among them.

The inheritance laws in France are in some way responsible for the confusion with wines and the amount of labels that are very similar. When the owner of a vineyard dies the estate has to pass to all the beneficiaries in equal parts, it cannot go to a sole beneficiary. This means that there are many small estates that produce wines of very different quality but with names that can be almost identical. The small estates mean small quantities and if it is a top quality wine this can lead to high prices as demand grows.

Culture

It wasn't until the late 18th century that Burgundy became part of France, before then it was reigned over by the powerful Burgundy Dukes. The history of Burgundy and wine stretches way back to Roman times when the Romans started planting grapes in the area. Tales of wine being produced in the region are in Eumenes' Discources in A.D. 312 and this appears to be the oldest written reference. In the Middle Ages the monasteries were put to good use as the monks made wine and sold it to the nearby towns and eventually to Paris.

By 1395 standards had been set for the Burgundy winemakers and in 1416 King Charles IV decided that the wine of the area was special and made clearly defined boundaries for the region. Agreements between traders meant that the wines of Burgundy could be enjoyed by other countries and supplies were sent by boat to Belgium and England. The French revolution in 1789 devastated many of the monasteries where the wine was made and the huge vineyards were divided into smaller parcels of land.

The Burgundy region has not one but five villages in **the prettiest villages of France** category as well as three World Heritage Sites and a very unique medieval building project. There are some fantastic events and festivals throughout the year to celebrate wine, history, art and life so you will be sure to find something to suit your taste.

Go along to the Parc de l'Arbre Sec in Auxerre and join in the three days of the Aux Zarbs musical mayhem. The open-air festival takes place in the middle of July every year and features singers and groups from all over France and beyond. For music lovers of a different kind there are jazz concerts the first three Fridays of August on the shores of Lake Kir. Southeast of Dijon the open air concerts of the D'Jazz à la Plage are for everyone, young and old.

For opera lovers there is the International Baroque opera festival in the town of Beaune as well as numerous other wine-related festivals in the same town. In the heart of the Puisaye to the west of Dijon is Château Saint-Fargeau. Every year there is a spectacular sound and light show with 600 actors taking part and enacting ten centuries of history in amazing and colourful pageants.

There is just so much to do and see it is hard to know where to start but the biggest theatre event in France takes place in the streets of Chalon-sur-Saône. The four day festival takes place at the end of July every year and performers come from all over Europe and beyond to take part in the Chalon dans la Rue (Chalon in the Street). Around 300,000 spectators come to witness the 1000 or so performances that take place in the streets and on stages. Puppets, clowns, acrobats and fire eaters; come and have a wander through the streets, you never know what might be waiting to surprise you round the next corner. Pop and rock is offered at the Alésia the Nuits Péplum event and the Festival of Words at La Charité-sur-Loire lets you join and use your talking talents. Lormes is home to the Festival of French Song and folk music at the Fête de la Vielle held in Anost.

Location & Orientation

The narrow Burgundy region starts one hundred kilometres southeast of Paris and stretches 360 kilometres south towards Lyon. In this 31,500 sq. km there are an amazing 1000 kilometres of canals. The Canal of Burgundy has 209 locks for boats to pass through. Canal barges and houseboats are available to hire and are a popular way of travelling through the region. Some of the locks have helpful and friendly lockkeepers while some locks are unmanned and need a little elbow grease to get through. Many years ago goods were transported by barge and you could have your possessions shipped from the United Kingdom all the way through France to the warmer climes of the Mediterranean.

Dijon is the capital of the Burgundy region and is also the centre of distribution and communications in the area. Dijon is just over an hour and half by high speed (TGV) train from Paris or a slightly more sedate train journey from Basel or Geneva.

There is no international airport in the Burgundy area. To fly to the south of the region it is better to use the Lyon Saint-Exupéry airport that is 68 kilometres from Mâcon or Geneva airport. The Paris airports are about 300 kilometres away. There is a small airport in Dijon that has scheduled flights to Toulouse and Bordeaux in France but not to Paris.

Road links are excellent with fast, smooth motorways going from Dijon in all directions.

Climate & When to Visit

The Burgundy climate can be kind; the summers are warm and pleasant and quite hot in July and August. Average temperature in summer is 19°C but the highest ever recorded was a staggering 38.1°C. Apart from these two months the summer night-time temperature can be cool, so be prepared with a jumper or jacket. One of the threats of the summer months is hailstorms and in 2009 a vineyard was destroyed in this way.

Autumn brings the grape harvest and for the three or so weeks the workers in the fields are bundled up to go to work early mornings and gradually peel off the layers as the hours go by and the sun comes out. Going home means wrapping up again as the chilly evenings set in.

Winter can be cold and the lowest temperature ever recorded was minus 21.3°C. The average though is about 1.6°C. The winters are usually a dry cold though, snow does fall but there is not the damp feeling in the air like in the UK.

Springtime can be nice as the cold of winter is going away with the promise of warmer days to follow. If you are lucky and get nice weather the area is wonderful as the flowers start to blossom and there are not too many people about.

For visiting in spring and autumn it can be wet, so maybe pack some long trousers and decent hiking boots, especially if you plan on doing much walking as the paths can get slippery. In winter wrap up warm, think thick gloves, furry hats and boots. If you get a chilly there is always plenty of wine to warm you up especially a nice glass of **vin chaud** (hot spiced red wine). Don't use the 1945 Mouton Rothschild or 1787 Château Lafite though!

Sightseeing Highlights

Beaune

Beaune is known as the Champs Elysées of Burgundy and is close to famous name villages known to wine-lovers such as Pommard and Gevrey-Chambertin. In the heart of the vineyards the town has much for the visitor to see in the way of heritage without even setting foot in a vineyard. Many people come to the town whether they are professionals or beginners to learn about the region and the wines that are on offer here.

The town has everything for a wonderful stay and the level of gastronomy is like the wines, from cheap and cheerful to top class; there are brasseries, bistros offering table d'hôte menus right up to Michelin star restaurants. As you stroll through the cobbled streets and gardens full of fragrant blooms you will come across mansions from a bygone age and half-timbered buildings that hide intriguing places to eat. With over a hundred restaurants there is something for everyone. Choose from jellied ham, snails or coq au vin and don't forget to try the local cheeses of Citeaux and Eoisses.

No stay in Beaune would be complete without a wine tour of some kind. Whether it is underground to the wine cellars and their hidden treasures or a journey out to a vineyard there are hundreds of ways of being introduced to wine. A lovely way to discover the countryside and pretty villages is by hiking. In and around Beaune there are 14 marked footpaths, with different lengths and degrees of difficulty, three of these footpaths pass through vineyards so why not stop off for a spot of wine tasting on the way.

Hospice de Beaune (Hôtel de Beaune)

Rue de l'Hôtel Dieu
21200 Beaune
Tel: +33 380 244 700

This delightful hotel is set in a former alms-house that was founded in 1443 for the poor and needy. A stunning example of fifteenth century architecture is the hospital building that is now a museum. Luckily now patients go to a more modern hospital. Every November an important charity wine auction is held here.

Notre Dame Collegiate Church

Place Général Leclerc
21200 Beaune
Tel: +33 380 247 795

Over the centuries various elements have been added to the original Romanesque architecture, gothic portals and a 16th century chapel and bell tower. There is a 12th century statue of the Virgin Mary as well as tapestries depicting her life.

Burgundy Wine Museum

Hôtel des Ducs de Bourgogne
Rue d'Enfer
21200 Beaune
Tel: +33 380 220 819
www.musees-bourgogne.org

You can find anything and everything to do with viticulture here in this magnificent setting. The Burgundy Dukes lived here for a few hundred years from the 13th century onwards and they have left behind a legacy of wine-related tapestries, art and tools for us all to learn from.

Dijon

Dijon is in an ideal location on the main road from Paris to Lyon. The Dukes of Burgundy lived in the province until the late 15th century and this meant that Dijon was a place with enormous wealth and power.

There are houses in the centre of the town that date from the 18th century that are still inhabited today; but hopefully they have some modern conveniences by now. The roofs of Dijon are one of the distinguishing features of the areas architecture with glazed tiles in geometric patterns and vibrant colours of green, yellow, terracotta and black. There are about 700 hectares of parks and green spaces and many, many museums that are worth a visit

There are many important fairs held in France but Dijon is home to the International and Gastronomic Fair every autumn. The fair is in the top ten of most important fairs in France and attracts 200,000 visitors and 500 exhibitors. The international flower show Florissimo is held here every three years.

We are all familiar with Dijon mustard which was invented here in 1856 when the juice of unripe grapes was substituted in the traditional mustard recipe. How many of us know that this is also where Crème de Cassis comes from. The blackcurrant liqueur is mixed with white wine to make the drink Kir.

Dijon Opera

11 Boulevard de Verdun
21000 Dijon
Tel: +33 380 488 282
www.opera-dijon.fr

Opened in June 1998 the Dijon Opera has the most beautiful acoustics in Europe and attracts major conductors and orchestras. Many productions are brought to life here, theatre, dance and performing arts. Have a look at the programme before you plan your trip, there might just be something you would like to see.

Museum of Burgundy Life

17 Rue Sainte-Anne
21000 Dijon
Tel: +33 380 488 090
www.musees-bourgogne.org

For an insight into Dijon life pay a visit to the Museum of Burgundy Life. The museum opened in 1982 and is in the cloisters of the Bernadine Monastery. The collections show possessions and costumes about Dijon daily life from the 18th century to the beginning of the 20th century.

Dijon Cathedral

6 Rue Danton
21000 Dijon
Tel: +33 380 303 933
www.cathedrale-dijon.fr/

The present Gothic cathedral was built between 1280 and 1325 and while not the most inspiring of cathedrals it is worth visiting while you are in town.

Owl's Trail (La Chouette)

If you are visiting Dijon with children, or without, take some time to follow the Owl's Trail round the town to see the sights. The trail is named after the owl on the façade of the Notre Dame church who you must stroke for good luck! The tourist office will have the English language brochure or hire an audio guide and go owl hunting.

Augustodunum Roman Theatre

Rue Maladière F
71400 Autun

The town of Autun was founded for and named after the Roman emperor Augustus when Augustodunum became his headquarters. The Roman Theatre here is huge and has a capacity of 20,000. It doesn't take much imagination to hear the roar of the crowds echoing down from the past. The theatre is free to enter and visitors can wander round at their leisure.

In late August everything changes and six hundred residents of the town come together to put on a spectacular display. The Roman theatrical show goes on for several hours and is good fun even if somewhat hard to understand. Take some blankets, cushions and drinks to make a day of it with the family.

Touro Park – Zoo

Maison Blanche
Romanèche –Thorins
Tel: +33 385 355 153
www.touroparc.com/

Touro Park might not be very big but it manages to pack 800 animals from 140 species into its 12 acres. The way the zoo is arranged means you get really close to the animals, safely of course, and see how they thrive in their home from home beautifully kept surroundings. See the white tigers, elephants, giraffes, lizards, rhinos and much more.

There is also an adventure park, a small train, monorail and an old fashioned carousel dating from 1900. Once you have seen the monkeys in the zoo why not go on the **Amazon Adventure** course and see how well you can imitate them as you swing through the jungle ropes. If you fancy a splash around after a hard day in the wilderness, there is a waterpark to cool off in. There is the Beaujolais Village and Museum, two snack bars, a restaurant and picnic areas and watch out for the souvenir shop on the way out.

The park is open every day from February 15th to November 15th.Summer hours are June 1st to August 31st 9.30am to 6.30pm and in the other months the park closes one hour earlier. The amusements open at 1.30pm each day. Adult tickets cost €15.50 to €19.50 and children €13 to €16.50 depending on the time of year.

Parc de l'Auxois – Water Park and animals

Route Départementale 905
21350, Arnay-Sous-Vitteaux
Tel: +33 380 496 401
www.parc-auxois.fr/

Parc de l'Auxois is far more than just an animal park. The 35 hectares have all the necessary attractions to make it a really good day out but the park is also there to educate. It is very important that every generation learns about the lifestyle of the animals and how some of them are under threat from mankind. Parc de l'Auxois plays an important part in working with other European parks and conservation organisations to protect conservation areas in Madagascar, French Guiana and Asian and African countries.

If any exotic pets are confiscated by the local authorities or not wanted by their owners they will be given refuge at the park. Turtles, ostriches, parakeets, monkeys, snakes and lemurs are all examples of the animals that have been taken in here.

For amusement there is mini-golf and playgrounds or you can take a train ride through the park. Find the maze and lose yourself, or the children, in the intricate patterns. You can wander across the suspension bridge and gaze down at the shady areas of the park and see if you can spot any of the animals taking refuge from the sun. There is a swimming pool and water games through the summer months so remember to bring your swimming costume.

There are places to eat, drink and juts relax and the park is open from 10am until 7pm every day. An adult ticket is €14 and children between 3 and 12 years old pay €10.

Muséo Parc Alésia – Interactive museum

1, route des Trois Ormeaux BP 49
21150 Alise-Sainte-Reine
Tel: +33 380 969 623
www.alesia.com

In 52 B.C the Gallic tribes with Vercingetorix as their leader fought Julius Caesar's Roman army at Alesia. The remains of the Gallo-Roman town can be found on the top of Mont-Auxois and several thousand people lived there over the first few centuries AD. There is a superb centre here where you can see the living quarters, how they made their crafts, the theatre and basilica etc.

The Interpretation Centre uses films, models, diorama and multimedia to plunge you into battle with reproductions of the war machines. The Roman fortifications have been built to their original height and stretch for around 100 metres. You can see daily life in a Roman camp reenacted before you as the cast of players recreate the training of legionaries and show manoeuvers and battle techniques.

The terrace around the Interpretation Centre is planted with silver birches and oaks and offers a 360° view of Mont-Auxois and the hills where the army camps of the Romans were set up.

There are audio-guides available in several languages, a souvenir shop with gifts and books and a caféteria. For children there are play areas as well as fun guides so they don't get bored. There are various ticket prices depending on which part of the site you wish to visit and the opening times change throughout the year. It is probably best to check out the website or give the site a call before you visit.

Morvan Forest

The Morvan Forest is in central Burgundy and was created in 1970 to conserve the natural environment. The park covers 2,800 km ^{2} and has just about everything anyone could wish for to make for an enjoyable outdoor life. There are six reservoirs for watersports, plus rivers and streams, some fast-running and some moving so gently you can hardly see the flow. Low mountains and woodlands hide tiny villages where the pace of life is slow and relaxation is easy.

Talking of relaxation, why not stay for a day or two in Bourbon-Lancy or Saint-Honoré-les-Bains taking the natural waters' and sampling the treatments available. Once you have been revitalized the walking opportunities abound on miles of well-marked paths. Even driving is less hassle on gently winding back roads where speed is unheard of.

A lot of the area is granite with some limestone towards the edge of the park and the area gets hot summers, cold winters and lots and lots of rain on the higher ground. The highest peak is just 900 metres but snowfall in winter can be harsh.

Treats include locally produced cheeses, hams and sausages and lime and acacia honey. The timber industry years ago was there with the sole purpose of keeping Paris warm. Today the timber is cut under strict rules and is used for the fine oak barrels for the vineyards.

One of the mysterious sounds of the forest is the cry of the stags in September as they call for partners. The moaning and wailing call echoes for miles and miles and the stags share the night with humans who are waiting to hear the call of the wild with them.

Wine Tours in Burgundy

www.authentica-tours.com/

A trip to the Burgundy region would not be complete without a tour of a wine cellar or vineyard, preferably both.

A typical basic half-day tour will take three or so hours leaving in the morning or afternoon. You will visit a wine cellar full of exceptional Burgundy wines. Accompanied by a choux pastry nibbles you will get to try red and white wines. You will also visit a wine estate in Gevrey-Chambertin that can trace its history for generations and try one of the best labels that Burgundy has to offer. Admire the immaculately kept cellars and barrels and sample Pinot Noirs that owe their flavour to tradition and local soil.

Similar half-day tours can be taken but with the addition of visiting local cheese factories and learn about the art of matching the right wine to the right cheese.

A seven hour full day tour is available that includes a private visit to a family run estate in Còte de Nuits. Follow the Champs-Elysées of Burgundy from Dijon to Beaune, stroll through vineyards and taste some of the Premier and Grand Cru white and red wines. In Beaune there is time for lunch (not included) and to visit some of the historical sights of this beautiful city.

The tour guides are chosen for their knowledge of the Burgundy area and the wines. They are all bilingual (English/ French) and will patiently answer any questions you may have. The guides are an excellent source of information for other places to visit in Burgundy and can advise on the best places to eat and drink.

Boat trips on the Burgundy Canal

www.european-waterways.eu/e/info/france/canal_de_bourgogne.php

The canal opened in 1833 and connected Paris to Burgundy and still is the shortest connection between the two. Although no longer used for transportation as parts of the canal are now too shallow with a draft of only 1,40 metres, it does make a wonderful cruising holiday.

The Burgundy canal might be one of the most pleasant to cruise though in France but there are some considerations to be made. The many locks will need some man-handling and if there is not a lock-keeper, are you strong enough? Reversing into a mooring space is not like parking the car, it is rather like trying to steer a reluctant elephant backwards into a small garden shed. Boats can be cramped, although beautifully fitted out, so if you are on the tall side watch your head! Having said that, messing about on the canal is a peaceful way to travel through this beautiful region and discover the many delights on offer.

Auxerre Cathedral

Place Saint-Étienne
89000 Auxerre
Tel: +33 386 522 329
www.cathedrale-auxerre.com/

Built between 1215 and 1233 this mainly Gothic cathedral is located over an 11th century crypt. Parts were still being added to the building as late as 1540 when a renaissance cupola was added to the completed tower. The cathedral is known for the massive stained glass windows and the three Gothic style doorways. The cathedral is well worth a visit to admire the carvings and mouldings and just to be in awe of the craftsmanship that went into the making of such a beautiful place.

The cathedral is only a very short distance from the river and there are pretty parks and plazas all around to wander through. There is parking right outside the door, if you are lucky, or down along the riverfront.

The cathedral opens every day at 7.30am and closes at around 5pm. The treasure and the crypt open an hour or so later. The cathedral may be closed on occasions for special functions or holidays. The price is €3 per adult for the cathedral and €2 for the crypt. Children under 12 are admitted free of charge.

Building a Castle at Guédelon

D955
89520 Treigny
Tel: +33 386 456 666
www.guedelon.fr/

For somewhere completely different take some time to visit Guédelon. While many of the chàteaus and castles in France are being restored using modern methods and technology this one is being built from scratch using traditional ways. Fifty craftsmen covering a range of trades including rope makers, blacksmiths, carpenters, woodcutters, stonemasons, quarrymen and tile makers have started to build a castle using only traditional Middle Age techniques and materials. All the necessary materials are being found on and around the site in an abandoned quarry

The brainchild of the owner of Chàteau Saint-Fargeau the project was started in 1997 and is scheduled for completion around 2020. Guédelon is open to the public and whether you are family on holiday or a professional wishing to learn about this time in history it is a pretty amazing place to see.

Imagine a construction site with no heavy machinery, no cement mixers, no drills and saws buzzing away to disturb the peace. Take a step back in time and hear the satisfying sound of stone being carved by hand as the stonemasons chip painstakingly away to make the perfect fit. There are no cranes to lift heavy materials skywards, just simple wheel and pulley systems and the size of the bellows at the forge has to be seen to be believed.

Château de Tanlay

89430 Tanlay
Tel: +33 386 757 061
www.chateaudetanlay.fr/

Château de Tanlay is beautiful and charming; there are no other words for it. The approach to the house is across a bridge over the moat and through a pair of obelisks standing guard. The moat surrounds the house apart from the one access and would have been instrumental in protecting the château from marauding intruders. The limestone walls enclose the courtyard with cylindrical towers on the four corners and the roofs are finished with typical French slate.

The 13th century foundations were built over in the 16th to 17th centuries by François de Coligny d'Andelot who inherited the ruined site from his brother. The château is still owned by the same family of the man who created the title Marquis de Tanlay in 1705. Tanlay is famous for in particular the trompe l'oeil painted gallery and the frescoes in the tower.

Visitors are welcome from April 1st to November 2nd, but not on Tuesdays. To wander the grounds only costs €3 and a guided tour of the interior to admire the beautiful artwork and furniture costs €9 for adults and €5 for children. The guided tour includes free access to the grounds. The tours begin at set times morning and afternoon.

Mustard Factory

Moutarderie Fallot
31 rue du Faubourg
Bretonnière
21200 Beaune
Tel: +33 380 221 002
www.fallot.com/

Mmmm, who doesn't like mustard on their ham sandwiches? The Mustard Mill of Fallot has been a family owned, independent Burgundy company since 1840 and it is the first museum in France to be dedicated to mustard. An interactive tour leads through a journey of the ages where you can learn about the making and history of mustard. The tour is great for beginners and will have your sense of smell tingling as you go round.

Mustard has been around a long time and some of the materials and ancient tools are displayed and along with a sound and light show reveal many of the secrets of the world of mustard. This a novel experience in Burgundy and if you wish you can practice being a mustard-maker quicker than you can say hotdog.

La Moutarderie Fallot originally made mustard grinding the mustard seeds with a grindstone and they have managed to preserve this traditional method but with the aid of modern technology can show you how the wild mustard seed becomes the condiment we all know and love.

The price of a visit is €10 per adult and €8 between 10 and 18 years old.

Château de Pierreclos

71960 Pierreclos
Macon
Tel: +33 385 357 373
www.chateaudepierreclos.com/

In the heart of the vineyards of southern Burgundy you will find the beautiful example of medieval architecture that is Château de Pierreclos. The entrance is guarded by two gatehouses, giving way to a sweeping driveway that leads to the house. The interesting tile pattern on the gatehouse roof is continued through to some parts of the main building.

The oldest parts of the château date from the 12th century and once you have entered through the pretty gateway you reach the terrace, the romantic Mâconnais vineyard and the Romanesque church. In the château make sure you visit the armoury and the spice room. The bakery and the kitchen are fascinating and will make you very glad that we live in an age of modern conveniences.

Nine centuries of history await you in this château in Burgundy. In 1989 a programme of renovation was undertaken by the Pidault family to allow the public access to share their beautiful home. Now the château provides venues for business or private events.

A visit to the château ends in the vaulted cellars with information about the wines and of course some samples of the wine they produce. There are various tours, guided or non-guided, plus wine tastings. The chàteau is in an exceptional location and once you have had your fill of history you can visit the shop and pick up a few bottle to take home to remind you of your visit.

There are several Burgundian specialties, treats and souvenirs and make sure you try the rosé and white sparkling wines or Crément de Bourgogne. There are fruit liqueurs available with exciting flavours like vine peach, morello cherry and Ratafia au marc de Bourgogne.

Tours, dates and prices are all available on the châteaus website or just give them a call to arrange the tour that suits you the most.

Recommendations for the Budget Traveller

Places to Stay

La Maison de Mireille

2, allée du Château
89800 Courgis
Tel: +33 386 414 671
www.la-maison-de-mireille.fr/

Less than 10 kilometres from the town of Chablis is the pleasant village of Courgis. Maison de Mireille is a small privately owned hotel that caters to just six guests and sits on the edge of the sleepy village. The pretty, romantically decorated rooms are well equipped with private bathrooms and comfortable beds and furniture. There is free Wifi and free parking.

The price is €50 per night for one person or €55 for two. This includes continental breakfast with locally made bread and preserves.

Comfort Hotel Beaune

58 Route de Verdun,
21200 Beaune
Tel: +33 380 241 530
www.comfortinn.com/hotel-beaune-france-FR395

The Comfort Hotel Beaune is just a short drive from the city centre and has 46 rooms all with private bathroom. Each room has flat screen TV, satellite channels, toiletries, hairdryer, a hospitality tray and microwave. The hotel has a restaurant and bar area, an outdoor pool and terrace, a laundry service, conference and business facilities, a play area and garden. There is free parking on site and free Wifi.

The price per room is around €70 per night depending on season and children under 12 stay free if sharing a room with their parents and no extra bedding is required. Breakfast is charged at €8.50 per adult and €4 for children.

Premier Class Avallon

Rn 6 - La Cerce, RN 6,
89200 Sauvigny-le-Bois
Tel: +33 892 70 72 51
www.premiereclasse.com/

The Avallon is part of the Premier Class chain and if you want budget accommodation you can't beat staying here. The rooms are impersonal, the soundproofing is not great but for a bed for the night when driving the long road north-south or east-west it makes an affordable stopping place. More of a transit hotel than somewhere to spend a holiday as there are no frills or charm but it serves its purpose. There is Wifi, vending machines and 24 hour access with a credit card so no restriction on arrival times.

A double room in the middle of June for two people costs just €28. Beat that! It is outside of the town right opposite the three star La Relais Fleuri, so don't get them mixed up.

Hotel Kyriad

35 Place De Beaune
71100 Châlon-sur-Saône
Tel: +33 385 900 800
www.kyriad.com/

The Kyriad in Châlon-sur-Saône is in the heart of the town right by a shady tree-lined plaza. The rooms are comfortably furnished with modern décor and a nice touch is a welcome tray full of goodies when you arrive. The rooms have private bathrooms, TV, hairdryer and free Wifi. Parking is easy right outside and the river and main attractions of the town are within walking distance.

There is an unusual bar / dining room with a natural stone curved ceiling and gaily checked tablecloths. Breakfast and other meals are available in the hotel. In August a double room will cost you €60 for two people.

Hotel Quick Palace

Rue de Bruxelles - ZA des Macherins
89470 Moneteau
Tel: +33 386 534 475
www.quickpalace.com/

Super easy access to the Quick Palace Hotel off the motorways N6 and A6 make this a good choice for overnight stays while travelling. Just north of the town of Auxerre and opposite thickly wooded areas the hotel has all you need for a comfortable night's stay. The rooms are soundproofed, have private bathrooms with toiletries and TV with satellite channels.

A self-service buffet breakfast is available from 6.30am each morning with a good selection of pastries, brioches, preserves, cereals, juices and hot drinks. The breakfast is a very reasonable €5.50.

A double room can be booked for around €30 depending on the time of year. There are some good offers on the hotel website, some with breakfast included.

Places To Eat & Drink

L'Antre II Mondes

21, rue d'Ahuy
21000 Dijon
Tel : +33 380 580 208
www.antre2mondes.com

If you are a fan of rock music and love medieval times then this is the place to go in Dijon. The atmosphere is great with huge wooden tables and grey walls decorated with medieval reminders. On Friday and Saturday lunchtimes there is a traditional folk atmosphere but in the evening the music turns into rock as the friendly owners play your favourite songs. The staff are friendly, they welcome families and if you want to eat at a unique restaurant, this is definitely it.

They serve excellent snacks and sandwiches as well as an interesting selection of historical and regional dishes. Choose from salads, a varied selection of meats cooked mediaeval style and you can wash it down with a glass of mead, or a pint of Mandubienne, a traditional Dijon beer. Prices start at €5 and they are open all day, every day.

La Cassolette

466 of Route Nationale 6
Creches sur Saone 71680
lacassolette.e-monsite.com/

The pretty pastel colours and friendliness of the charming gentleman owner makes this a very worthy stopping place in the Macon area. If your French is not great he will help you in his very best English without making you feel silly. This is an excellent restaurant and there really should be more like it.

The freshly cooked dishes all use local ingredients so the menu is very regional. There is a three course daily menu which is excellent value at €14.50 which includes a starter, a warm main course and a choice of local cheeses or dessert.

Au Bureau

5 rue de Beaudelaire,
71100 Chalon-sur-Saone,
Tel: +33 385 482 801
www.aubureau-chalonsursaone.fr/

Right in the centre of the town and by the railway station Au Bureau is open all day, every day and there is always something happening. Poker nights, concerts, theme nights and all the big matches live make this a very popular place to go.

The menu is very different with many of the dishes served on slate, there are exciting meat platters, huge burgers and a good selection of other items to tempt you. The dessert section looks very good so make sure you leave some room. The daily menu is €10.

The Publican Pub

44 rue Maufoux,
21200 Beaune
Tel: +33 380 207 622

This is a good English pub/restaurant. The prices are very reasonable for food and drink and the wines they serve come from the owner's in-laws. The seating is great with lots of comfortable couches and chairs and there is a terrace for a drink in the sun. They serve platters of meats, cheese and fish and you won't leave feeling hungry. Prices start at just €3.

Les Café Des Amis

18, rue Carnot
21500 Montbard
Tel: +33 380 920 060

Cheap, friendly and colourful is the best way to describe this café. The owner decides the dishes for every day and one day it can be a delicious chicken curry, the next a big pot of stew. They always use the best seasonal produce so the menu varies throughout the year.

The main dish of the day is €7.50 or the three course daily menu is €11.50. When you have finished your meal have a game of cards with the owner, he is more than willing to sit and chat with you. The bar is open to welcome you every day of the week.

Places to Shop

Flea Market

Place des Fontaines
89600 Saint-Florentin
Tel: +33 386 351 186
www.saint-florentin-tourisme.fr

Take a wander around a French flea market or **brocante** as they are known locally. Hunt out some old, or not so old, French treasures. What could be better than a Sunday morning rummaging through old boxes searching for hidden goodies? Afterwards find a bistro and enjoy a glass of wine, Burgundy of course.

Saint-Florentin is just one of many markets. There are big ones and small ones held all over France, some only March to October and some all year round. There are also major markets at Aillant-sur-Tholon and Mézilles.

Shopping in Beaune

http://www.beaune-tourism.com/

There are 500 shops in the centre of Beaune that will cater to your every need so it is very difficult to choose just one. Half the fun of shopping in another country is wandering round window shopping and browsing, so make a day of it and then visit one of the many places to eat for a spot of lunch. Parking is easy as there are 5,000 spaces to fill in and around the area.

Many of the streets are pedestrianised, the shop windows are colourful and beautifully decorated and the shopkeepers are polite and professional and only too happy to help. Every other shop seems to sell wine or wine related articles so finding a good vintage or two shouldn't be difficult. There are a multitude of delicatessens, arts and craft shops, a wine library, clothes and shoe shops and plenty of banks to get the necessary spending money from.

Cluny, Carrots and Chocolates

Saône-et-Loire
Burgundy

Cluny has a marvellous outdoor market on a Saturday morning. There is so much locally produced food you won't know what to buy first. Cheeses made from goat's milk, organic vegetables and fruits, gingerbread, homemade pâtés and of course plenty of wine. There are also clothes, wickerwork and some furniture.

Cluny also has one of Burgundy's great chocolate producers; Germain-Au Pêché Mignon is family run and you can taste the most exquisite handmade goodies. There is very sensibly a tea-room and café for trying the delicious pastries inside the century old cake shop that the family have transformed.

Wine Shopping in Beaune

Avenue Charles de Gaulle
21200 Beaune
Tel: +33 380 240 809
www.vinscph.fr/

For the past 25 years the owners of La Grande Boutique Du Vin in Beaune have worked with local wine growers who have small or medium size vineyards. The selection of wines to choose from is vast with over 1000 different labels. The white two-storey building doesn't betray from the outside the treasures hidden within and the wooden shelves hold rows and rows of neatly displayed bottles and boxes. The staff are always ready to help and quite happy to let you taste the wines before making the all-important decision of which one, or ten, to buy.

Galeries Lafayette

41 – 49 rue de la Liberté
21000 Dijon
Tel: +33 380 448 212
www.galerieslafayette.com/

Galeries Lafayette is one of the biggest chains of stores in France and the stores are usually in magnificent old buildings that have been around for hundreds of years and Dijon is no exception. The building itself will take your breath away with the carvings and mouldings on the exterior. Mingle with the elegantly dressed French ladies as they glide through the many floors taking their time over what to buy. There is fashion, food, jewellery, perfumes, shoes and household goods to browse through. Visit the caféteria to rest your weary feet once you have shopped until you drop, or just to leave the menfolk in while you go round a second time! Opening hours are generally Monday to Saturday. 9.30 am to 7.30 pm.

Welcome to Strasbourg & the Alsace Region

Alsace (Pronounced Al zass) is one of the tiniest and most densely populated provinces in France. Located in the upper east corner of the country, Alsace shares its borders with Germany and Switzerland. The Upper Rhine River cuts across its eastern border and the Vosges Mountains lie to the west.

The word Alsace is derived from an Old High German word meaning "foreign dominion." It's an apt word for this small parcel of land. From as far back as the Roman Empire, Alsace has found itself an unwitting pawn in the game of empire building. Great armies have swept across this land in search of the treasures and wealth found in Paris. WWII was particularly destructive as many of its priceless cathedrals and castles were destroyed.

This tug-of-war resulted in Alsace effectively becoming its own region within the Republic of France. Its capitol, Strasbourg, is a hub of political activity. Dozens of international organizations are based here making it the one of the most important regions within the European Union.

The country is quite small. It is 190 km long and 50 km wide. Packed within this tiny area are nearly 2 million people.

The region has always been known for its fine wine. Roman soldiers returning from this area spoke highly of the quality of wine they found here. Today wine remains one of the top reasons visitors flock to this area. The 'Route de Vin' is a small road that connects the wineries and vineyards with cities and towns.

Alsace is a particularly beautiful part of Europe. Castles and ruins dot the hillsides. Though heavily damaged, the towns retain the old European look and feel lost in so many contemporary cities. Given its history as a stepping-stone to lands beyond, tourists will find nearly as much German influence as French. Restaurants serve some of the finest sauerkraut and beer found outside of Germany.

Alsace has much for the tourist to do. In addition to wine tasting, the picturesque countryside makes for delightful sightseeing and day trips. Many excellent museums are here detailing the history of this area. The food is diverse and particularly good.

Alsace is a unique pocket of Europe.

Culture

The history of this area is one of seemingly endless struggle. Nomadic hunters roamed this area in pre-historic times. In 56 B.C. Romans settled here and began making precious wine it would ship back to Rome to be consumed by the nobles and elite. As the Roman Empire collapsed, the Holy Roman Empire took its place where it remained a seat of power until the Protestant revolution of the 16th century.

Always in the crosshairs of the marauding armies of France, Spain, Holland and Germany, the Alsace region came under French control in 1639.

By the 18th century, Alsatians were expressing a similar discontent and desire for autonomy and self-rule as the people of surrounding France were. When word reached Alsace that the walls of Paris's hated Bastille prison had been broached and citizens seized control, riots broke out and eventually the grip of feudalism overthrown.

Throughout the first half of the 20th century Alsace bounced between German and French control. Following WWII the region was taken over by France in whose hands it remains today.

For most of its history Alsatian was spoken. This is a language similar to the German spoken in Switzerland. Today French is the dominant language.

The Germanic influence is most notable in the old style architecture and food. While newer construction is entirely French, the older sections look very much like an old town in Germany. Fires were a frequent occurrence during the time of the bubonic plague. In order to facilitate the construction and reconstructions of homes, houses were made of timber framing and the floors were made of stone. Timber framed houses are also easy to knock down and reconstruct. This was particularly helpful in the past as the Rhine was subject to frequent flooding.

Alsatians are well known lovers of food. German influenced meals dominate the menus. A particular favorite is a form of sauerkraut known as Chouroute. When you visit Alsace be sure to leave your dieting at home as the meals here are notoriously plentiful.

The German influence is also evident in the region's libations. The area is well known for its white wines especially the dry Rieslings. Hops are grown in the northern part of the country and many fine breweries are found throughout the country, particularly around Strasbourg.

Given its turbulent history, Alsace has taken on symbolic importance as a place of hope where pan-European alliances can be formed. In 1949 Strasbourg became the seat of the Council of Europe. Today the European Parliament is here.

Alsatians are known as warm and convivial people. Their joie de vivre is particularly evident during the holidays which they celebrate with great enthusiasm. Their welcoming spirit is a delight for travelers looking for a place to slow down and relax a bit. If you're looking for beautiful scenery you can explore while dining on fine food and wine, Alsace may be just what you're looking for.

http://www.region-alsace.eu/region-alsace/discovering-alsace-region

Location & Orientation

France consists of 27 regions. Alsace is the fifth smallest. Alsace lies slightly south and to the east of Paris at a distance of 379 km (235 miles). Across its southern border is the Swiss city of Basil. 456 km (283 miles) directly east of Colmar is Munich Germany.

Travelling to and around Alsace is quite easy. Major roads link the area to the rest of France as well as Germany and Switzerland. Europe's fine rail network links the region with the whole of Europe and beyond. Tourists can also arrive on a boat running the Rhine River. Alsace is the most cycle friendly area of France. 2000 km (1242 miles) of bike paths crisscross the countryside. Three EuroVelo routes pass through the area.

Climate & When to Visit

Winters are notoriously harsh in Alsace. Thanks to the nearby Vosges Mountains, very little snow and rain falls here. Winter highs range between 4-6 c (40-47 f). Nights will fluctuate between -0.1 and -0.3 c (30-33f). Spring months find the days ranging between 11 and 20 c (52-68 f) and nights vary between 2 and 9c (36-49f). Summers are mostly sunny and the daytime temperatures fall between 20-25c (68-77f). Nighttime hovers between 12-14c (55-58f). The start of fall finds the daytime temperatures starting at 21c (69f), and falling to 5c (41f) in December. Nights start at 10c (51f) and will drop to 0.3c (32f) when winter starts.

Sightseeing Highlights

Strasbourg

http://www.otstrasbourg.fr/?lang=en

Located in the Eastern part of the Alsace region near the German border is the capital city of Strasbourg. Given the changing political fortunes of the area, Strasbourg has long been a prized pawn. Strasbourg itself is a French and Germanic name. Stras is derived from the German Strasse, or street. Bourg is a French word which means Burg in German and borough in English. Strasbourg roughly means the 'fortress on the street.' This harkens back to a time when the city was of exceeding geographic and economic importance. Goods traded between the east and western parts of Europe had to pass through the fortification of Strasbourg.

In addition to being the seat of the European Parliament, Strasbourg also hosts numerous other European institutions including the European Court of Human Rights, the European Ombudsman of the European Union and the Central Commission for Navigation of the Rhine.

In 1988 UNESCO classified the entire city center as a historic city Center. This was the first time in history UNESCO bestowed the honor on an entire city.

Every the hybrid of French and German cultures, this coexistence extends to its tolerance of religions as well. The city plays host to a large number of people of the Catholic and Protestant faith. In November 20012 the Strasbourg Grand Mosque opened. It is the largest Mosque in France.

In addition to the beauty found in the Alsace region, Strasbourg is within easy distance of some spectacular scenery. The city lies on the Upper Rhine River Basin along the Ill River. Across the border in Germany, the Ill flows into the Rhine. 25 km (16 miles) to the west is Germany's beautiful Black Forest. This Black Forest is so named because it thick carpet of conifers block out all of the sunlight.

The forest is renowned for its many hiking and biking trails. Deep within the forest the headwaters of the Danube can be found. Cutting across its hills are the continental divide. On its western side water will flow into the Rhine River and out to the Atlantic Ocean. On the eastside water will flow into the Danube and empty into the Black Sea. Within easy driving distance from Strasbourg are found some of Europe's finer examples of old cities that date back hundreds of year. Among these are Staufen, Haslach, Calw and Freiburg.

Wine connoisseurs who want to take a break from tasting French wines will find a wonderful tour running from the south to the north of the Black Forest. Perhaps the greatest exports to come out of this region are its clocks. The clock making industry somewhat died out following the first and second world wars but these legendary clocks are still on display. A circular route that takes you around the forest stops in all the little towns where the craft of clock making was turned into an art. The clock tour is not often on the radar of many tourists, which is a pity. They are really quite amazing and worth the time to take the tour.

20 km (12 miles) to the west are the Vosges Mountains. With Switzerland so nearby, calling the Vosges 'mountains' might be a bit of a stretch. They are more like the undulating hills found in the nearby Black Forest. Of particular interest is the Northern Vosges Regional Natural Park. Listed by UNESCO as one of world's international biosphere reserves, the park is one of those places of untouched beauty. All manner of forest and fauna are found here. Numerous animals including deer and lynx call the park home. 1,650 km of hiking and biking trails crisscross the park. In an area of such unique beauty, the park stands out as a particular favorite for tourists visiting the area.

The Vosges Mountains were one of the most contested areas during WWI. This annexed area was a matter of national pride for France. In 1914 both armies dug in and waged a war for possession of this parcel of land that lasted over a year. The battle effectively resulted in a standoff. Each side dug itself ever deeper into the ground by building enormous trenches and encampments dug into the granite. Remains of these can be found to this day.

The city itself is often considered one of the most beautiful in the world. Within the city are numerous attractions to delight the tourist with some of the finest attractions found in Europe.

One of the favorite walks is through a neighborhood known as Le Petite France. Known as the French Quarter, this is a city that remains as it was when built during the middle ages. As you walk among its cobblestones you can take in an ancient city that is all but lost as progress marches on. This is a high rent section of town. It is where you will find the finest dining the city has to offer as well elegant shopping.

The Musée Alsacien or Alsatian Museum located on 23-25 quai Saint-Nicolas, is dedicated preserving artifacts from pre and early industrial Alsace. This an excellent place to visit if you want to get an idea of what life was life in simpler times.

An interesting garden is the Botanical Gardens located at 28 Rue Goethe. Unlike the well-manicured gardens found in Japan or Victoria B.C., Strasbourg's Botanical Gardens are somewhat overgrown and left to nature to cultivate as she sees fit. Because of this the garden plays host to not only a large variety of plants but is home to numerous insects and amphibians as well.

Amid a city of cobblestone streets and medieval architecture sits the ultra-modern European Parliament. Located at Allee du Printemps, the building is quite noticeable from far away. Visitors are welcome when Parliament is in session. If you wish to see this, be sure to plan your trip accordingly. The website is www.europarl.europa.eu/ Once there you must call ahead to assure yourself a seat. The phone number is 33 (0)3 88 17 20 07

Another art museum that is a favorite for visitors to Strasbourg is the Musee des Beaux-Arts. Taken from a poem by W.H. Auden and translated as the Museum of Fine Arts, the museum houses one of the largest collections of art by the Dutch painter, Pieter Bruegel the Elder. What are most appreciated by visitors are the detailed explanations that accompany the works of art. Rather than featuring a name, title and date, works here are accompanied by explanations of the work, its meaning and its place in the larger context of the times in which they were painted. The museum is located at 2, place du Chateau.

Later will be an explanation of a wine tour you can take around the Alsace region. But if you're in Strasbourg and looking for a place to start your excursion, the Wine cellar of Strasbourg city Hospital is an excellent place to visit. Located in the basement of the city's hospital at 1, Place de l'Hopital, the wine cellar has been in use for over 600 years. The wine cellar does not advertise itself and can be a bit difficult to find. To find it go to the medical hospital at the Civil Hospital. When your there walk through the main gate and the entrance will be the first door on your left. You are free to visit it at your leisure. Tours are also available that will give you a good idea on what types of wine you will find around the region. If you would like a tour, call ahead at 33 3 88 11 64 50 to find out when they are available.

One final attraction in the city itself that will give you a good idea of the history of the area is the Musee Archeologique , Strasbourg's Archeological Museum. Located at 2, place du Chateau, the museum is an old style museum that looks like a gothic cathedral. Headsets are available to will walk you through the exhibits. Here you will find excellent examples extending back as far as the Neolithic and Roman occupation. Other works follow the history of the area right up to the present day. If you're spending a night or two in Strasbourg before heading out to explore the countryside, a visit to this museum will give you a good idea of the places you will be visiting and its history.

Kammerzell House

16 Place Cathedrale, Strasbourg
+33 3 88 32 42 14
http://www.maison-kammerzell.com/accueil_en.php

The Kammerzell House sits atop what was the headquarters for the Holy Roman Empire. First built in 1427, the building went through renovations in 1467 and 1589; it remains a masterpiece of German Renaissance architecture. The house was for civil purposes. Because of this it was constructed in the traditional black and white timber framed style.

The interior, with its sumptuous display of frescos by Leo Schnug is on display to the public. The house now features a restaurant.

Strasbourg Cathedral

Place de la Cathedrale
67000
Strasbourg, France
+33 3 88 32 75 78
http://www.strasbourg.info/cathedral/

Known as the Cathedral of Our Lady of Strasbourg, construction on the cathedral began in 1015 and was completed in 1439. Over the years poets and writers have marveled at it beauty. Victor Hugo called it a "gigantic and delicate marvel." Goethe, with his better sense of poetry, called it a "sublimely towering, wide-spreading tree of God." At 142 m (466 feet) was the tallest cathedral in the world until it was superseded St. Nikolai's Church in Hamburg Germany. Today it remains the sixth tallest cathedral in the world. So tall is it that it can be seen across the entire planes of Alsace. Its spire is visible from the Vosges Mountains in France on into the Black forest in Germany.

Throughout history the land upon which the cathedral sits has been used as a place of worship for a number of different religions. The Roman emperor Nero Claudius Drusus established a military outpost across the Rhine River. On the site of Strasbourg Cathedral his army made camp calling the area Argentoratum. Over the years this place burned six times. The emperor Trajan laid the foundations upon which the modern church sits was first established.

Over the years construction has continued. Each successive building built on the last but added modern touches to the building. A walk around the cathedral gives a fascinating glimpse into the various architectural styles that have gone into its construction. Along its southern transept are found examples of 13th century statues and sculptures. Of particular interest is the 'Pillar of Angels' featuring a depiction of the Last Judgment.

Around the cathedral is evidence of its Romanesque style. Later cathedrals would place great emphasis on high windows with colored glass depicting biblical scenes. The Strasbourg Cathedral features much more ornate and intricate walls than those found on newer ones. Of particular interest is the west front. Carved in the Gothic period, thousands of scenes and figures are carved into its walls. It is a stunning testament to the ingenuity and craftsmanship of Gothic artists. It cannot fail to move anyone with even a passing interest in art. For a religious person it seems divinely inspired and is a place of veneration and worship.

Like all great works of art, Strasbourg Cathedral has been a beacon to those of ill intent. In June of 1940, Hitler visited this spoil of war and declared it to be a shrine for the German people. Later the stained glass windows were removed and hidden in a salt mine in Heilbronn Germany. In August of 1944, British and American bombers carpetbombed the area with the intent of driving the Germans out of France. The Cathedral sustained significant damage that was not fully repaired until the late 1990's. More recent times have seen a cell of Al-Qaeda bombers intent on blowing up the cathedral and a nearby Christmas market, broken up by French and German police.

Hunspach

http://www.tourisme-alsace.com/en/272000057-Hunspach.html

This beautiful little town is located in the North Vosges Natural Park. The German influence is very much in evidence here as the houses are built in the Alsatian half-timbered style. Primarily a farming community, Hunspach is one of those delightful European villages that exist nowhere else in the world. Hunspach is frequently referred to as one of the most beautiful villages in France.

Mont Sainte Odile

http://www.mont-sainte-odile.com/?lang=en

Named after Saint Odile, daughter of Adalrich, Duke of Alsace, this spectacular monastery/convent sits atop a 760 m (2500 foot) peak in the Vosges Mountains.

This site has been a place of veneration and worship for as long as humans have occupied the area. Evidence of Neolithic and Celtic settlements has been found in the surrounding area. The Romans used the site to construct a strategically placed fortress from which they could look down upon invading armies. In 407 their luck ran out as Vandals overran the fortress and leveled it to the ground. By the 10th century most Europeans had converted to Christianity. It was then that Vikings attacked and swept across the Low Countries. The seat of power for church officials and bishops at that time was in Utrecht. Sensing a grim future, the bishops fled in exile and took up residence at Mont Sainte Odile. The building was destroyed during the Middle Ages and rebuilt in the 17th century.

One of the great works of Christian literature the Hortus Deliciarum or Garden of Delights was written and illustrated by Herrad of Landsberg was written here in the 12th century when it was known as the Hohenburg Abbey. At its time it was a veritable encyclopedia of all that was known.

One of the more notable features of Mont Sainte Odile is the 'Pagan Wall.' Why and when it was built is a matter of some dispute. It seems undeniable that the wall was constructed as a way of keeping marauding invaders at bay. The structure circles Mont Sainte Odile at a length of 10 kilometers (6.2 miles) at a height of 3 meters (9.8 feet) high and a width of 1.8 meters (5 feet 11 inches). Legend has it that the wall was originally constructed by Druids more than 3,000 years ago. Of late, scholars date its construction to the 7th century and attribute its name 'Pagan Wall' to Pope Leo IX.

Colmar

Colmar is another of those uniquely beautiful cities in the Alsace region that deserves a visit. It is one of the stops on the wine tasting tour that will be discussed in a bit. If you're not making a wine tour the city makes for a relaxing day stroll.

Located between Strasbourg and Basel, Colmar is a medieval town that has preserved much of the architecture and charm from those times. While some recent construction has gone on, the old town has remained intact and is where you will find all of its attractions.

Of all its old buildings none is more beautiful than the Maison des Tetes or House of Heads. This wooden house was built during the Renaissance. Now a hotel, the Maison is best known for its interesting carvings of faces and heads that adorn the building's façade.

Nearby is the St. Martian Church. What makes this church so interesting is that it is colored pink. Visitors to the Strasbourg Cathedral will have noticed that a part of its exterior is also pink. The color of the stone is found only in a particular spot in the nearby mountains.

Lying at the entrance New York City's harbor is the Statue of Liberty. What most people don't realize is that the statue was a gift from the French. The sculpture of the iconic American statue was a man from Colmar named Frédéric Auguste Bartholdi. In Colmar there is a museum named the Bartholdi Museum that is dedicated to his life and work.

Of particular pride for the citizens of Colmar is the Unterlinden Museum http://www.musee-unterlinden.com/ The museum houses a unique collection of Alsatian art. In addition to paintings, the museum has an exquisite collection various types of furniture and everyday household items used by Alsatians of years past. Also found are paintings by Renoir, Holbein the Elder and Picasso.

Little Venice is a collection of canals found in the old part of Colmar. In times past the canals were the way produce and goods were ferried around the city. Today a scenic boat ride along the canals is a relaxing and unique way to view the medieval charm of Colmar.

Château du Haut-Koenigsbourg

67600 Orschwiller, France
+33 3 69 33 25 00
http://www.haut-koenigsbourg.fr/en

Here is another stop on the wine route that is well worth a visit by itself. The chateau sits high in the Vosges Mountains and commands a sweeping view of Alsatian plain. When it was first built is unknown. The first references to it are found in the 12th century.

In this land of such strategic importance, the little spur of land upon which the chateau sits has been a hotly contested bit of real estate. During the Thirty Years War the chateau was overrun by the Swedish army who ransacked and all but destroyed it. Its obvious beauty and haunting ruins were the inspiration for many of the leading romantic poets and painters.

On the eve of the 18th century, Bodo Ebhardt was commissioned with the task of rebuilding the castle to what it was prior to the Thirty Years War. Using what plans he could find, Ebhardt worked for 8 years to restoring it to its former glory. He did his job exceedingly well and the chateau has remained one of the most popular tourist sites in France. In 1993 the French Ministry of Culture designated it as a national historic site.

Mulhouse

http://www.mulhouse.fr/en/

Mulhouse is the second largest city in the Alsace region behind Strasbourg. Located in the eastern part of the region it's close to the borders of Switzerland and Germany.

Its founding is unsure. The earliest written record of its existence dates from the 12th century. The city itself is steeped in myth. Local legends tell of a city dating back to the first century B.C. At the height of the French Revolution the Treaty of Mulhouse was signed and control of the city was taken over by France until the Franco-Prussian War of 1870. At that time it came under German rule as part of the Alsace-Lorraine territory. The city essentially remained in German hands until the area was returned to France in May 1945.

Industry in Mulhouse consisted mainly of textiles. Throughout the 19th century the city enjoyed a lively trade with the state of Louisiana. Bales of cotton poured into the city fueling its burgeoning textile industry. Later the city would become a hub for engineering and textile industries. Today it has branched to electronics and automobiles. The largest employer in Alsace is the Peugeot factory in Mulhouse.

The city is divided into four districts. The Rebberg district was built on the wealth of Louisiana cotton. Originally this was the heart of wine production. Rebbe is German for 'Vine.' The layout of the town was constructed to resemble that of Manchester England with houses built on terraced steppes.

The Nouveau Quarter (New District) is the expensive part of the city. After the stone walls were torn down in 1826, work began on developing a carefully orchestrated layout for the city. The precision of its streets are a model that should serve as a template for cities built today.

The Lower Town is where the artists, craftsmen and merchants are to be found. This area is for pedestrians only and makes for a delightful walk and day of shopping.

The Upper Town has been under construction for 300 years now. This part of the city is where the majority of religious institutions are located. Many monasteries are found here. Throughout the years this section has hosted Augustinians, Franciscans, Knights of Malta and Poor Clares.

Palais Rohan

2 Place du Chateau,
67000
Strasbourg, France
+33 3 88 52 50 00
http://www.musees.strasbourg.eu/index.php?page=le-palais-rohan-en

The Palais Rohan, or Rohan palace, is one of the more interesting sites in all of Alsace. In an area known for it rich and varied architecture, Palais Rohan stands alone. Built in the early part of the 18th century, it is a masterpiece of Baroque architecture. Commissioned by by the King's architect Robert de Cotte, the building first served as the residence of Cardinal Armand-Gaston de Rohan-Soubise, Prince Bishop of Strasbourg. Its style was to mimic and one up the Parisian homes of the wealthy and elite. Through the years other notables have taken up residence here. King Louis XV stayed here in the middle of the century, while the ill-fated Marie Antoinette lived there in 1770. Napoleon Bonaparte lived here in the early years of the 19th century and added some rooms for his comfort and that of his wife.

Today the building is noted for its collection of museums. In its basement is the Archeological museum. The ground floor hosts the Museum of Decorative Arts. On its first floor is the Fine Arts Museum.

Even if you've become a bit weary of museums by the time you reach Strasbourg, the building is worth a look. Its high facades and exquisite interior faithfully preserve the time it was built. It looks as if you've stepped into a set of a Hollywood movie - but it is all real. Step inside and realize that this was the residence of many people who occupied it during some of the most turbulent times in French history - it is almost a sublime experience.

Alsace Wine Route

http://www.vinsalsace.com/en/

http://en.wikipedia.org/wiki/File:Weinbau-frankreich-elsass.png

The Alsace Wine Route is one of those famous places not to be missed by connoisseurs of fine wines. In recent years Australia and America have begun producing world class wines. Tours through the southwest corner of Australia, California and Washington State are a treat of fine wines, good food, comfortable surroundings and convivial company but they lack that certain something a tour through wine's old country has. The vineyards are soaked in history.

You feel the love and craftsmanship of generation's vintners who worked the soil, tending to the grapes through good times and bad, and celebrated their fortunes with friends and family over good meals, much laughter and fine wine. It's also quite amazing to think that Romans took up residence here to grow grapes, produce wine, drink themselves silly as soldiers are want to do, and ship the rest back to Rome where it was consumed by emperors, nobles and statesmen.

Alsatian wine is primarily white wine. The region is particularly famous for its dry Rieslings. Another favorite are the Gewürztraminer wines. Like much else about this region, the wines produced here are heavily influenced by German wines. Wines here are tightly controlled by the Appellation d'Origine Contrôlée or 'controlled designation of origin.'

Three main types are produced. Alsace Grand Cru AOC is for white wines produced at certain locations. Crémant d'Alsace AOC is for sparkling wines. Alsace AOC is for red, rosé and white wines. The wines here tend to be very aromatic. As mentioned earlier, early wine production was influenced by German tastes.

With political and geographic autonomy, wine makers have exhibited a similar zeal to produce wine with a unique Alsatian stamp on them. Initially this led to growers to produce very dry wines. Lately wine makers are producing wines with residual sugar in them. Pinot Gris and Gewürztraminer wines are often produced this way. Muscat, Riesling and Sylvaner wines tend to be much dryer. The Alsace region also produces some excellent desert wines. Because of this, traditional wines may not be quite what you're accustomed to.
Alsace wines are produced along a small strip of land. This topographical map will give you a good idea of the wine country and surrounding terrain:
http://en.wikipedia.org/wiki/File:Alsace_topo.png

The mountains on the west are the Vosges Mountains. Alsace is subjected to westerly winds most of the time. The mountains provide ideal protection from storm fronts passing through that would deluge vineyards with rain. The region ranges between 175-420 meters (600-1,400 feet). With the dry conditions and plentiful sunlight, conditions are ideal for wine production. The best of the wines are produced out of the shadow of the Vosges range on the south-east and south-west slopes.

The wine route of Alsace is called the Route des Vins d'Alsace. This well-marked road runs from north to south. This 170 km road passes through 67 communes. Many more wineries are found along the way. There are so many places to sample wine and have a meal that it would be impossible to do them justice here. While there are favorites that stand out among visitors, it would be impossible to give definitive locations. An excellent website that contains a wonderful map and is stuffed with useful information is: http://www.alsace-wine-route.com/en/alsace-wine-route-and-cycle-route-map/ The bottom line is that this is an area best left for you to explore.

Whether by car or on bicycle, the Route des Vin d'Alsace is a place that rewards the curious. If locals have one bit of advice it is that you avoid the popular spots. By doing so you will find a place much less crowded where you can relax with a glass or two of wine, enjoy a sumptuous meal and take in the breathing beauty of the Alsace region. Travel rewards the curious and if you take time to explore you will find a number of quaint places just off the beaten path where you had the finest wine, meal, company and views of anywhere you have ever visited. The best advice to visiting this area is to do some homework. Get a feel for the land and its towns, then just get out and explore.

Another option is the many tour companies that will take you to the most popular destinations. Tour companies will take you to the best spots. Knowledgeable guides will inform you of what you are passing along the way. If you do choose a tour company, look around the internet and see how it is rated by those who have used it. This will give you a good idea of its reputation.

Recommendations for the Budget Traveler

Places to Stay

Hotel Kyriad Mulhouse Centre

23, Rue des Trois Frontiers
68111 Illzach

+33 3 89 61 81 50
http://www.kyriad.com/en/hotels/kyriad-mulhouse-nord-illzach

The Kyriad are a chain of three star hotels found throughout France. This particular one is chosen because it lies at the beginning of the wine tour. Mulhouse is one of Alsace's more popular cities and is known for its many museums and tourist attractions.

This hotel has 47 rooms, each with a private bath. 2 rooms are specially designed for people with limited mobility. The hotel has a restaurant and bar. The chef is well known for preparing local meals that are in season.

Its location is ideally suited. The airport is a 20 minute drive away. Major roads intersect in Mulhouse making excursions into Germany and Switzerland quite easy.

Rooms begin at 50€.

Hotel des Vosges

3 Place De La Gare
67000 Strasbourg
1-866-539-0066

Conveniently located near the train station, the Hotel des Vosges in been in existence for over 100 years. Much of the hotel is built in the style found in the years just prior to WWI. A particular favorite for travelers is its Breakfast Room. This has the look and feel of an old style Alsatian tavern with a fireplace blazing away. An excellent restaurant is open for all meals.

Within easy walking distance are the Strasbourg Cathedral, the Notre Dame Museum and the Alsatian Museum.

All rooms are smoke free. Dogs are allowed in the rooms. Bathrooms have all necessary amenities. Rooms have a television with cable access. Wireless internet access is available for a surcharge.

Rooms start at 65 €.

Aux Trois Roses

7, Rue de Zurich
67000 Strasbourg
00 33 (0) 3 88 36 56 95
http://hotel3roses-strasbourg.com/UK/index.php

This is a hotel that is preferred by backpackers and travelers who think hotels are a place to drop off you stuff, go out and explore, crash for the night and get up and do it all again. It is a bare bones place with little of the luxuries and comforts found in more expensive hotels.

While it is not the sort of place you would want to spend a few days resting after a bought of sightseeing, it is not a shed either. The Aux Trois Roses has a sauna and a sunken Jacuzzi. A breakfast area serves breakfast for a surcharge. Its 32 rooms feature minibars. All rooms have tubs and showers. Wireless internet access is available. Rooms have a LCD television with satellite connection.

The hotel is strictly non-smoking. Violators will be fined.

Rooms start at 77€.

Ciarus

7 Rue Finkmatt
F-Strasbourg
+ 33 (0) 3 88 15 27 88
http://www.ciarus.com/

The Ciarus is a hostel located in the center of Strasbourg. It is one of those places that appeals to younger travelers, including the backpack and hitching crowd. It is a loud, noisy boisterous hostel that seems to bustle with activity 24 hours a day. It is a wonderful place to meet travelers who have arrived from all points far and near.

The Ciarus has 290 beds in 101 rooms. Rooms range from single beds to double beds to rooms with bunk beds. All rooms have a private toilet, sink and shower. Wi-Fi internet access is available. The reception area is open 24 hours and has a wealth of material for travelers on their way across Europe.

Rooms start at 21€.

Hotel du Rhin

7, place de la Gare
6700 Strasbourg
+33 3 88 32 35 00
http://hotel-du-rhin.fr/?lang=en

Built during the reign of Kaiser Wilhelm II, this cozy hotel is a steal. Its rooms are tastefully decorated and give a warm feel. Many rooms have excellent views including the new and impossible to describe train station.

The staff is multi-lingual and is available to answer any questions you may have. In addition tours are run from the hotel. If you wish to make a day excursion around the cities and neighboring area or book a wine tour, you can do so at the front desk.

All rooms have a private bath. Wi-Fi internet access is available. Satellite TV is available in all rooms.

Rooms start at 71€.

Places to Eat and Drink

Au Koïfhus

2 pl. de l'Ancienne-Douane

Colmar, 68000
03 89 23 04 90
www.restaurant-koifhus-colmar.fr

A well-known spot for locals, this restaurant features traditional meals from the Alsace region. Among its specialties are coq au vin with spaetzle, crayfish and grapefruit salad choucrote colmarienne served with a variety of different meats. A meal should cost between 12 and 15€.

Zum Strissel

5 pl. de la Grande-Boucherie, Strasbourg
67000
03 88 32 14 73
www.strissel.fr

It's not often you get to eat at a restaurant that first opened its doors in the 1500's. The Zum Strissel is a unique dining experience. The interior is decorated to reflect the rich history of the area. Meals are most traditional fare. Baeckoffe and Choucroute served with pike perch are particular specialties. Its bar is richly stocked with a wide variety of Alsatian wines. If you want dinner in an old-fashioned location where you can relax and sample some of the best wines the area has to offer, the Zum Strissel is a perfect stop.

Meals cost around 15€.

Au Tire-Bouchon

29 rue du Général-de-Gaulle
Riquewihr,
68340
03 89 47 91 61
www.riquewihrzimmer.com

One of the most popular places around, the Au Tire-Bouchon is frequently filled with customers. If you would like to dine here it is recommended you call ahead to book a table. Of all the places mentioned, this is the one that tries to make its meals uniquely authentic. In addition to meals mention in other places, here particular attention is paid to seasonal game dishes. This is definitely note fare for those who think of meat as steak and hamburger. A seasonal meal also consists of local produce. What makes the Au Tire-Bouchon stand out is its selection of local wines. This may very well be the place where you can sample the widest variety of Alsatian wines.

Meals start at 13€.

Le P'tit Cuny

97 Grand-Rue, Vieille
Ville, Nancy
54000
03 83 32 85 94
www.lepetitcuny.fr

Food here is more from the Lorraine tradition. This is another one of those locations that is constantly stuffed. The tables a placed close together and the atmosphere is constantly busy as wait staff rush about serving customers.

Le P'tit Cuny has a reputation for serving hearty meals at reasonable prices. Traditional meals can be found here as well as such exotic items as foie gras-stuffed pig's trotter and calf's head.

Meals cost around 15€.

Places to Shop

Christmas Shopping in Strasbourg

Legend has it that the first Christmas tree was put on display in Strasbourg. Whether this is true or not is a matter of some debate. What can be said for sure is that the Christmas market in Strasbourg was founded in 1570. It is considered to be the finest Christmas market in all of Europe. Certainly travelers from large cities will be taken aback by the traditional atmosphere where mechanized Santa's and neon lights are not to be found.

Open from mid-November through December, the Strasbourg Christmas market is not just a place where merchants sell their wares. With the harvest season just ending and the dark days of winter settle in, the market place becomes a festival dedicated to the season. Shoppers can stroll from chalet to chalet sampling freshly baked deserts and libations. Events take place all the time. Singers, bell ringers and puppet shows will delight the entire family. Needless to say every trinket and bauble related to Christmas can be found here. Shopping at Strasbourg's Christmas market is an experience like none other.

La Fromagerie Saint-Nicolas

18, rue Saint-Nicolas
68000 Colmar
+33 (0)3 89 24 90 45
www.fromagerie-st-nicolas.com

Much has been made of the wine produced in this region, and for good reason. What is often overlooked is the high quality of cheese produced here. Of all the cheese makers in the region none is more famous that this one. Run by the same family for years, their cheese is most likely what you will be served in nearby restaurants and on display at local farmers markets. Travelers recommendations of this shop are plentiful and consistently rate it with four and a half and five star ratings.

BURGUNDY & ALSACE TRAVEL GUIDE

Bookworm

3 rue de Pâques Town Station
03 88 32 26 99
www.bookworm.fr

This is not one of those megastores you can get lost in
throughout the afternoon. Instead it is an ideal place for a
traveler to find books to help orient him to this great
region. If you find yourself in the Alsace region and in
need of much more detailed information about the land
around you, the Bookworm stocks the books that will
help you find what you need. Travelers making 'The
Grand Tour' and in need of informative books on what
lays beyond will find helpful books to plan their trip as
they make their way out of Alsace and off to places
unknown.

Atac Supermarket

47 rue des Grandes Arcades Grand Ile
Strasbourg

It is not uncommon to come to this area and find themselves somewhat unprepared. Its wide open spaces, many hikes, pleasant vineyards and warm weather just cry out for a picnic. It's not often a traveler will pack a basket, cheese knife, blanket and cork screw opener. If you find yourself in the area and feel the need to spend a romantic afternoon or two taking in the beautiful scenery on a lonely hillside while dining on cheese and wine, you will find what you need at the Atac Supermarket. Of course you can find all the groceries if you want to stay in and make you meals where you are staying. But what makes this place special is that it caters to the picnicker. If you find yourself wanting to spend an afternoon under the sun enjoying the day, the Atac Supermarket will have the little knick-knacks you need but just couldn't stow in your luggage.

Chamonix

176 Rue Joseph Vallot
74400 Chamonix
00 33 4 50 93 52 73
www.chamshop@hsd3.fr

Chamonix is one of the stops along the world ski tour. It's trendy, upscale clothing is most likely not on the list of places for the budget traveler but if you're in the market for some of the finest ski attire to be found, things that will make you stand out at the slopes next winter, you can do no better to drop into Chamonix's and see if they have what you're looking for.

Printed in Great Britain
by Amazon.co.uk, Ltd.,
Marston Gate.